Difficult People
Dealing With Almost Anyone

Jennifer Rozines Roy

Enslow Publishers, Inc.

40 Industrial Road   PO Box 38
Box 398   Aldershot
Berkeley Heights, NJ 07922   Hants GU12 6BP
USA   UK

http://www.enslow.com

Thanks to Gregory Roy, Julie DeVillers, Desiree Palmateer, Amy E. Rozines, Virginia Quinby, the girls of P3, Cindy Anton, Daphne Chan, Sam Rozines, and Quinn Rachel.

Library of Congress Cataloging-in-Publication Data

Roy, Jennifer Rozines.
    Difficult people: dealing with almost anyone / Jennifer Rozines Roy.
      p. cm. – (Teen issues)
    Includes bibliographical references.
    Contents: What is a difficult person? — How difficult people can make you feel — When parents are difficult — Difficult school situations — Difficult people — they can be everywhere in the workplace — Getting along with a difficult person.
    ISBN 0-7660-1583-1
    1. Interpersonal relations in adolescence—Juvenile literature. 2. Interpersonal conflict in adolescence—Juvenile literature. [1. Interpersonal relations.] I. Title. II. Series: Teen issues
    BF724.3 .I58 R69 2001
    158.2—dc21
                                            00-009782
                                                CIP

Printed in the United States of America

10 9 8 7 6 5 4 3

To Our Readers: We have done our best to make sure all Internet addresses in this book were active and appropriate when we went to press. However, the author and the publisher have no control over and assume no liability for the material available on those Internet sites or on other Web sites they may link to. Any comments or suggestions can be sent by e-mail to comments@enslow.com or to the address on the back cover.

Illustration Credits: Wendy Edwards, pp. 13, 16, 24, 33, 39, 46, 53, 55; Robin Quinby, pp. 9, 43.

Cover Illustration: Portrait by Ed French; Background © Corel Corporation

Contents

1

What Is a Difficult Person?

Difficult people are everywhere. They come in all types—male, female, young, old, rich, and poor. Some people are more difficult than others. That can make them difficult to get along with. Sometimes a specific situation causes a person to react badly. Everybody has a lousy day or a bad moment once in a while, but difficult people seem to have them more often. And they do not seem to handle them as well as the average person.

Difficult people are people who do not behave toward others with politeness and respect. They choose to act on their feelings, whoever they hurt, instead of dealing with them in healthier ways.

There are two basic types of difficult people—*overt* and *indirect*. Overt difficult people are aggressive. They shout, rant and rave, and bully others to get their own way.

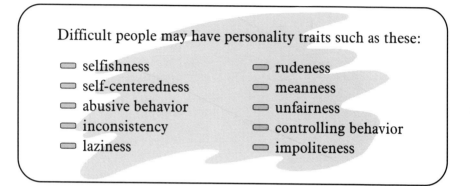

Difficult people may have personality traits such as these:

- selfishness
- self-centeredness
- abusive behavior
- inconsistency
- laziness

- rudeness
- meanness
- unfairness
- controlling behavior
- impoliteness

My father and I don't agree on anything. He sees everything differently than I do, and he refuses to even listen to my side. He screams and threatens me. If I don't do things exactly the way he wants it, things between us only get worse.

Julie, age 17[1]

Indirect difficult people are more passive. They duck responsibility, use people, and try to make others feel guilty. They do not attack others directly, but manipulate them to get what they want.[2] Whichever method difficult people use, the result often makes those around them miserable.

My girlfriend plays mind games. She cancels our dates at the last minute, then she gets mad at me for complaining. Sometimes she acts like she loves me and other times she gives me the silent treatment for no reason. She's driving me nuts.

Zackary, age 14[3]

Dealing with a difficult person can be, well, difficult. What makes it worse is that there are so many kinds of difficult people and each one may respond differently under different circumstances. A bully might use her power to scare other kids. A backstabber might act nice to someone's face but say mean things in his absence. A know-it-all may

I was having a really bad day. From waking up late, to missing the bus, to bombing a surprise quiz. The cafeteria even served my least favorite food, and I had to buy it because I hadn't had time to make a lunch. So there I was eating a sloppy joe, which I hate, and the kid sitting next to me spilled a little bit of soda pop on my tray. I mean it was really no big deal, but I blew up at him. I screamed names at him. Then I dumped his whole can of soda on his lap. I totally lost my temper over this tiny little thing. Everyone thought I was such a jerk.

David, age 16[4]

insist she is always right. And a hothead may simply explode with rage.

Even though they usually do not say it, every difficult person's message is similar. If other people do not do what he wants, the difficult person's attitude or behavior will only get worse. A difficult person wants his or her own way and instead of working *with* others to get it, the difficult person will work against them.

Sometimes a difficult person's methods will work. The people around him or her may simply give in so as to avoid further problems. Other times, however, the bad behavior is not effective. It just labels the person a pain, a jerk, or a "bad" person.

Why Do Some People Act Badly?

Nobody ever really knows what another person is going through. It can be hard to tell from a person's outside what is going on inside. That is why it is not always easy to figure out why a difficult person behaves the way he or she does. There could be many different explanations. Sometimes, as in David's case, the person is having a bad day and a specific incident triggers the unpleasant behavior. In other cases, the problem could be deeper and more complex.

A difficult person could have an unhappy home life. When members of families do not treat each other safely or with love, kindness, respect or honesty, the family is not functioning as a healthy unit. People with dysfunctional families often do not learn healthy ways of dealing with other people. Some examples of family situations that contribute to a difficult person's problems could be:

- divorced or separated parents
- single-parent households
- abuse
- alcohol or drug addiction
- overworking
- unemployment
- mental or physical illness

Any of these conditions can be difficult to cope with. A person who acts badly at school or at work may be reacting to something at home. However, it is important to recognize that not all people who grow up in dysfunctional families become difficult people. Many are perfectly nice, happy people! A difficult home life is not an excuse for a person to behave badly. It may be a reason for the behavior, but it does not excuse a person from the consequences.

There are many other things that contribute to a difficult person's bad behavior. Depression or anxiety can affect a person's responses. Alcohol, drugs, and even certain foods cause mood changes. (Sugar, for example, can sometimes make a child hyperactive.) Hormonal changes in women

The world would be a more pleasant place if there were fewer difficult people.

My parents split up when I was twelve. My mom worked really late hours, and I was left alone a lot. I started drinking and shoplifting. I started hanging out with kids who caused trouble. I laughed at my old friends for doing "lame" things like studying and going to church. After I ended up in juvenile detention and started talking to a counselor, I realized how much I was hurting about my parents. I blamed them for ruining my life, but now I know that I was really the one who was ruining it. I had made the choice to do stupid things. I could have studied or gone to church. I could have asked for help. My parents could have been better parents, but now I'm working on becoming a better person regardless of what they did.

Amy, age 18[5]

can also cause mood swings. In some cases, a difficult person may have a mental illness such as schizophrenia or bipolar/manic-depressive disorder. In extreme cases, a person might be a sociopath. A sociopath will hurt, abuse, or even kill without feeling guilt afterwards.

Most difficult people do feel some shame about their behavior. When they do something wrong, they probably feel bad about it. But their sense of shame may not be strong enough to force them to change their behavior. Other emotions—excitement, feeling powerful, and being in control—allow them to continue being difficult.

The feelings of being stressed-out, misunderstood, and confused are universal. People with different personalities handle these feelings in different ways. These feelings seem to happen more often and more intensely in teenagers. They are a part of adolescence. This is one reason teenagers as a group are often labeled "difficult." But difficult people

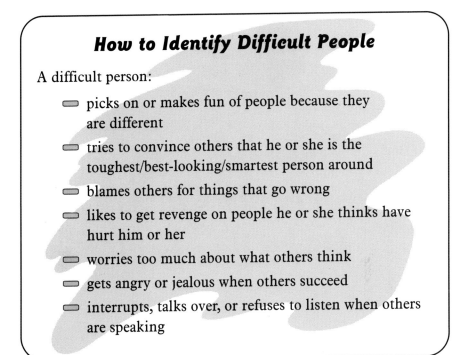

How to Identify Difficult People

A difficult person:

- picks on or makes fun of people because they are different
- tries to convince others that he or she is the toughest/best-looking/smartest person around
- blames others for things that go wrong
- likes to get revenge on people he or she thinks have hurt him or her
- worries too much about what others think
- gets angry or jealous when others succeed
- interrupts, talks over, or refuses to listen when others are speaking

can be all ages, just as there are nice people of all ages. Sometimes it takes only a few seconds to tell if someone is a difficult person, and sometimes it takes a lot longer. However, one thing is for sure—it is never easy to be around a difficult person when he or she is behaving in a difficult manner.

2

How Difficult People Can Make You Feel

Dealing with difficult people is never easy. There are many emotions that can arise when a person behaves in a way that causes problems. Difficult people can make other people feel frightened, confused, embarrassed, or depressed. These feelings are caused by a sense of helplessness. When a person seems to have control of a situation, others may feel powerless to change it. A difficult person is one who tries to take and keep control of a situation, regardless of how others feel.

> *I've been scared to get on the school bus lately. There's this kid who teases me and threatens to beat me up. Every weekday morning I wake up with a stomachache. On weekends I think, "Thank goodness—I don't have to face him today."*

> Hector, age 13[1]

My boss at work embarrassed me in front of the customers. Yesterday, she called me an idiot for not counting the change properly. I know my face was bright red, and the customer looked like she felt bad for me. But she's my boss. What could I do?

Katie, age 18[2]

My boyfriend drinks too much and he gets really moody. I never know if he's going to be in a great mood or a rotten mood when I see him. It's so confusing!

Shenise, age 18[3]

It is normal to feel anger toward a difficult person. Who would not be mad when somebody else acts difficult? The

Difficult people can make other people feel frightened, confused, embarrassed, or depressed.

first thing to realize is that it is okay to feel angry. The second thing to understand is that the way people handle their anger makes a situation better or worse.

I feel very angry when someone treats me badly. I feel like I want to scream or cry. I feel mad at myself for getting upset, because I'm only ruining my day by letting someone's meanness get to me.

Amy, age 18[4]

How to Deal With Anger

Anger has a useful purpose. It provides information that a person can use if he or she takes the time to figure out what needs attention. Then anger can be turned into helpful and meaningful communication. The best way to use anger is to let it out safely as soon as it is noticed. Early on, there is a smaller amount of anger to let out. Otherwise, it could build up and explode.

A girl in my class teased me a lot. For a long time I didn't do anything about it. I thought it would be easier just to say nothing. But inside I got more and more upset. So finally I couldn't take it, and I blew up. I screamed all sorts of names at her. Then I got in trouble for disrupting the class! I wish I had talked to her or told my teacher when it was happening instead of keeping quiet. I ended up yelling and looking bad.

Dylan, age 16[5]

Safe Steps to Expressing Anger

There are several ways to calmly express anger. These steps include:

- taking a deep breath and exhaling before speaking
- keeping perspective—making sure not to overreact

- maintaining a quiet, steady voice
- using polite words
- trying to solve the problem that triggered the anger

Positive use of anger gets results. However, if both parties involved in the situation are angry, a conflict can result. Conflicts can either tear apart a relationship or help it grow stronger.[6] When people safely express anger, there is often a resolution to the problem. But when they let their tempers get out of control, an argument can result. People want to be heard and understood, and if no one is listening, the conflict only gets worse.

Avoid an Argument

If at all possible, try to avoid an argument or fight. Here are simple steps to keep a disagreement under control:

- use appropriate body language—do not stand too close or step forward (called the challenge position), do not shake a fist or point a finger
- focus on similarities rather than differences—talk about what both sides do agree upon, use words like "we" and "us" rather than "you" and "I," find a common goal
- be honest—apologize for mistakes or misunderstandings and offer to make changes
- talk about the person's behavior, not his or her personality
- take a time-out from each other and let things cool off

A fight is a conflict in which someone ends up getting hurt.

What can be done to prevent a disagreement from escalating into a full-blown argument? When one person treats the other with respect and really listens, things tend to calm down. A disagreement with no yelling, threats, cursing, or name-calling will remain a disagreement, instead of turning into a fight. A fight is a conflict in which someone ends up getting hurt either emotionally or physically or both. It can be really hard to avoid fights with difficult people. However, an important lesson in dealing with these people is that there usually are ways to take control of the situation when somebody tries to start an argument.

The goal of resolving a disagreement is to find a common purpose and work toward reaching it. Any reaction that draws people closer is a positive step toward fixing the problem.

Occasionally the differences between two people seem too overwhelming. When arguments continue to occur between people, it is a sign that the problems are not getting better. The people in the situation may feel too angry, upset, frustrated, or confused to handle the conflict. Sometimes the feelings are so strong that one or both people want to hurt each other. When this happens, the only solution is to involve a third party. Another person is needed to help. This person should be objective. An objective person is somebody who does not take sides but listens to both people and helps solve the problem.

Objective third parties can include teachers, religious advisors, peer mediators, and counselors.

It is important to get help before an argument goes too far. Conflicts that grow out of control can be dangerous. If there is any threat of violence, help should be called for immediately.

Our youth group has a "Conflict Resolution" plan. If two people have a problem, they have to follow this process.

1. Talk it out. If they cannot work it out between them, they must try step 2.

2. Go to the group leader and explain the problem and then come to an agreement to fix the problem.

It is the kids' responsibility to get support so that the group can keep functioning. Everyone can have fun instead of worrying about fights. I think that's smart.

: David, age 16[7]

3

When Parents
Are Difficult

Parents—can't live with them, can't live without them.

Zackary, age 14[1]

I know my mom and dad love me, and I love them back. But it's definitely not always easy to like them. I've heard that teenagers are supposed to be difficult, but why do I think my parents are the difficult ones?

Cindy, age 16[2]

No one has ever had perfect parents.[3] Every grown-up has good moods and bad moods. Sometimes these changes in emotional state are due to outside influences, such as having a bad day at work or car trouble. Other mood swings have a physical cause, such as early morning grumpiness or fatigue from stress or illness.[4]

Parents can get bad-tempered when they are tired, unhappy, or impatient. They also may act in ways they learned from their own parents, writes Eda LeShan in *When Kids Drive You Crazy—How to Get Along With Your Friends and Enemies*.[5]

Different adults handle parenting in different ways. There are many parents who are able to communicate with their children and treat them fairly. Others have difficulty relating or being consistent. The style of parenting contributes to a family's functioning.

Parenting Styles

The various types of parenting styles can be defined as follows:

- *Authoritarian*—Parent(s) demand obedience and punish disobedience.
  Result: Child becomes fearful or resentful and may rebel.

- *Permissive–indulgent*—Parent(s) allow child to do what he or she wants and give things to make child happy.
  Result: While there is very little conflict, children who get their own way can become lazy or spoiled, or they may get into trouble with too much freedom. Eventually these children lose respect for the parents.

- *Permissive–neglecting*—Parent(s) are preoccupied with their own lives and are unaware of what their child is doing and where he or she is.
  Result: The child feels unwanted and unloved and misbehaves to get attention.

- *Permissive–firm*—Parent(s) give the child freedom to experience the world but also set firm limits.
  Result: The child experiences trust and affection and learns boundaries on behavior. This parenting style promotes healthy families and secure children.[6]

I'm sixteen, and my parents still treat me like a baby. I'm ready to make my own decisions and take control of my life.

Cindy, age 16[7]

My mother annoys me. She says I should grow up and make my own choices, but when I do, she either tells me I did the wrong thing or punishes me! I admit it's hard for kids to let go of their parents and hard for parents to let go of us. But it has to happen. That's what growing up is about, isn't it?

Peter, age 18[8]

As children become teens, families have to adjust to new situations. A power struggle between teens and their parents often results. Teenagers want to be out in the world experiencing everything, while parents want their kids to be safe.[9] It is the parents' responsibility to teach their children how to behave so that they do not hurt themselves or others. Parental discipline often includes punishment. Sometimes children feel that their parents are being unfair, when the adults are really trying to guide and protect their children. Punishments are reminders of what is acceptable and what is unacceptable. However, to the child, it is often the punishment that is unacceptable.

When small children are disciplined, they whine, cry, and throw temper tantrums. They do not, however, have the skills to argue their side. Teens have developed the ability to reason and debate. They often show off their developing skills by arguing—especially with their parents.[10] While constant battles are a sign of deeper problems, a reasonable amount of parent–adolescent conflict is not only normal but helpful. A teen who feels secure arguing with his or her parents without losing the relationship is learning important lessons. People often test their beliefs and learn who they are by bumping up against others who have different beliefs.[11] Becoming a mature, thinking adult means observing the parents' positions, keeping those ideas that they agree with, and rejecting those with which they do not agree.

A 1998 nationwide poll of 13–17 year olds conducted by *The New York Times* and CBS News found that 55 percent of the teens said there were times they had something they wanted to talk to their parents about but did not do so. Of these, four out of five said the reason was that their parents would not understand. The rest replied that their parents were too busy.[12]

Teenagers complain that their parents do not understand them. This is partially true. Adults look at things from a grown-up point of view, so they do not always realize the everyday stresses today's teenagers face. Grown-ups sometimes forget that peer pressure, grades, and boy/girl relationships are very stressful.[13]

So, when discussions come up regarding these issues, there may be communication problems and misunderstandings.

My boyfriend wants me to spend the weekend at his house while his parents are out of town. It's not like we're gonna do anything, just hang out. But I can't tell my father. He'd freak out. He doesn't understand what it's like to be my age. So I'll tell him I'm sleeping over at Amy's house, and she'll call me at Brion's if he needs me.

Daphne, age 19[14]

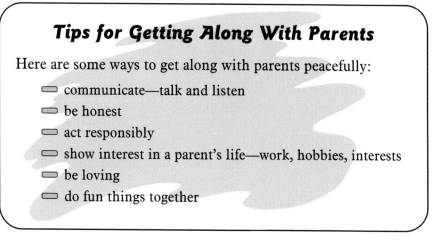

Tips for Getting Along With Parents

Here are some ways to get along with parents peacefully:

- communicate—talk and listen
- be honest
- act responsibly
- show interest in a parent's life—work, hobbies, interests
- be loving
- do fun things together

"Hot" topics families fight about:

- friends
- dating
- curfew
- money
- alcohol
- sex
- school

The bottom line? Teenagers can be difficult; parents can be difficult. If each listen to each other and respect each other, the parent–teen relationship will be much less difficult. Sometimes a parent is unable or unwilling to work on the relationship. When this is the case, a teen should look for support, advice, and role models elsewhere. A "surrogate" or substitute parent can be another family member (such as a grandparent or aunt or uncle), a teacher, or a community leader. If a teenager truly tries to get along with a parent who remains difficult, the young person must accept the reality of the situation and not blame himself or herself.

Help! My Parents Are Driving Me Crazy!

Here are some ways parents can be difficult, along with some ways to deal with them.

The Embarrassing Parent

There is a time in all teens' lives when they cannot help but dislike how their parents look and act. Embarrassing parents may wear the wrong clothes, talk too loudly, or treat their teens like little kids. And they do it in public.

Despite what their children may believe, what parents do is not a reflection on the kids.[15]

> *When I'm out with my dad in the mall and he starts acting weird, I am so embarrassed. So far, though, nobody has ever said, "Look at that guy. His kid must be a loser."*

> Hector, age 13[16]

Teens with this type of parent should talk to the parent in private and discuss their concerns. If the parent chooses not to change, that must be accepted. Parents are individuals with the right to their own personalities. Young people can explain to their friends that their parents are "behind the times" and realize that the other parents are probably embarrassing their own kids, too.

The Old-Fashioned Parent

This parent relives the "good old days" and tends to complain about the present by saying, "When I was a child, we never . . ."

When talking with a reminiscing parent, a considerate response is to listen. Older people like to tell children about their lives—it makes them feel important and that they are heard. A parent who longs for the past may wish for the security of those times. Their teens could be guided by the moral lessons of these stories. However, if the stories drag on too long or occur too often, it is okay to change the subject.

An "embarrassing parent" may wear the wrong clothes in public.

The Worrier

It is natural for parents to worry about their children. But parents who worry too much do not understand that their main purpose is to prepare their children to be responsible and self-sufficient when they grow up. Instead, these parents think their job is to protect their children from the real world.

Parents are justified when they worry. The world can be unsafe. But fears should not get in the way of a child's development. Excessive worry is not rational or logical, and it is not easy for a teen to reason with a worrier. It is wise for a teenager to try to show worrying parents that he or she is behaving carefully and responsibly. In addition, enlisting another adult to talk to the parents about their fears can help. A family member, clergy person, or counselor may help a parent cope with anxieties.

The Nag

Nagging parents say the same things over and over. They may nag about curfews or cleaning or doing chores. After a while, their family members get tired of them and tune them out.

> *My parents yell at me to do the dishes and take out the trash and walk the dog. What am I? Free labor?*
>
> Shenise, age 18[17]

The typical teenager's response to a nagging parent is "Yeah, yeah, whatever." This usually means, "I am not listening to a word you are saying." The truth is, maybe the parent nags because the teen is not doing what needs to be done. The best response is to repeat what the parent says, so that it is clear the teen has heard correctly. Then, the teenager should just do it . . . the first time.

The Angry Parent

A parent who has a bad temper can take it out on his or her child. Sometimes the anger can be a result of something the child does. Sometimes the child is a random target—somebody to yell at when the adult is upset with someone else. An angry parent yells and issues commands. He or she can be intimidating and loud.

An appropriate response to an angry parent is a calm one. Yelling back never solves the problem. A teenager can look his mother or father in the eye and say "What do you want, and why are you shouting?" in a respectful tone. That may be enough to quiet the situation. However, a parent may be so angry that he or she gets out of control. When this happens, it is best to leave the situation and get support. A young person should never be ashamed or afraid to tell someone that he or she needs help. In extreme cases of angry parenting, there may be abuse, and that should *never* be handled alone.

The Critic

Critical parents never seem satisfied with their children. They complain, insult, and put them down.

Young people whose parents focus on the negative rather than the positive should first try to talk about the problem with them. If this does not work, teens in this situation can surround themselves with supportive people, such as friends and teachers. Being around uplifting people keeps self-esteem intact.

The Pushy Parent

Parents whose dreams and ambitions were not fulfilled want to give their children the opportunities they missed.

My parents are awesome, but my best friend's home life isn't great. Her parents are on her all the time, and they can be really mean. She's counting the days until she turns eighteen, then she's out of there. I tell her: Hang on to your dreams and keep your chin up. When she's legal she can relax and make her own rules. For now, she's just gotta hang in there.

Quinn, age 15[18]

They may push their child to succeed at activities the child is not interested in or good at.

Teens who are pushed need to remind their parents that they are raising a child with his or her own talents and abilities. If the parents insist that they have a better perspective and will not back down, the teens may have to accept that participation in the activity will keep peace in the family for now, and that continuing calm discussions may improve things in the future.[19]

My stepdad wanted me to be a great baseball player, but I st[a]nk. I wanted to be on my computer. Then I had a brilliant idea. I got my stepdad to coach the Little League team. He was so psyched to be around baseball, that he let me sit in the stands with his laptop!

Dylan, age 16[20]

Neglectful Parents

Self-centered adults choose to spend their time and energy away from their kids. Even when their children try to get their parent's approval and attention, the parent remains distant.

Teens whose parents neglect them need to find other people who can give them attention and affection. Friends' parents, relatives, youth groups, and school clubs can be sources of support. It cannot hurt, of course, to talk to the parent about needing more time together. But if this is a longstanding problem, facing the reality that the adult may simply not be able to meet his or her child's needs will help a teenager move forward.

The most difficult parents are those who have serious problems that are beyond a child's control. Examples of this kind of parent include:

- alcoholic/drug abuser
- mentally ill person
- adulterer
- incarcerated person
- gambler
- violent abuser

Teenagers whose parents have those problems need to:

- get educated about the problem
- get help from a trusted adult (other than the parent)
- get to a safe place
- tell themselves that they are *not* responsible for their parents' problem

I've learned that I can accept my mom the way she is without liking or approving of what she does. I've learned to stop waiting for her to change. I've learned to ask for help. I've learned I have the right to be angry. I've learned that my mom drinks and uses, but I'm not my mom, and I won't.

Cindy, age 16[21]

4

Difficult School Situations

$\mathcal{S}$chools are not immune to difficult people. In fact, cramming hundreds of young people into a building day in and day out inevitably leads to some conflicts. Students and teachers have different personalities. Although they may not always get along with each other, they need to learn to get along in order to maintain a positive and healthy school environment. Young people have a right to feel safe, secure, and protected within their school community.

Bullies

Bullying is the first form of violence children usually experience. Eighty percent of middle-school students reported experiences with bullying behavior. Being bullied can destroy a kid's well-being and confidence.[1]

Students have always been involved in conflicts. But today, young people are quicker to resort to violence to get what they want.[2]

Bullies are people with problems. They like to be in control by hurting and frightening people they perceive as smaller and weaker. Bullies threaten, insult, tease, sexually harass, call names, spread rumors, give dirty looks, and beat people up. Being picked on by a bully is unpleasant. The truth is that no one—neither the victim nor the bully—is happy about such experiences. The bully almost always has been feeling hurt long before the bullying takes place. The meanest child, laughing the hardest at other's misfortunes, may be even more unhappy than the child he or she is being mean to.[3] Bullying incidents are serious and should never be ignored. Taking action is an important step

Steps to Stop a Bully

- Speak to a grown-up.
- Put all incidents down in writing and give to school administrators.
- Work on appearing self-assured—stand up straight, look people in the eye, hold head high, and talk with a firm voice.
- Do not go places alone and avoid areas the bully likes to go.
- Use humor to get the intimidating person to laugh.
- Remember that running away from a bully can be the smart thing to do. There is nothing shameful or cowardly about leaving a potentially dangerous situation.

toward feeling less frightened and abused. Both the victim and the bully need adult support. A person who is being bullied should speak to school authorities and his or her parents. Together, they can come up with an effective plan to solve the problem in a safe and appropriate way.

Cliques

Young people in school often form cliques. Cliques are groups of kids with similar attitudes and values. Cliques can be positive experiences when they promote healthful habits such as good grades or abstinence from drugs or sex. But cliques that purposely exclude others, engage in dangerous behavior, or pressure their members to conform are unacceptable. Kids who belong to these kinds of cliques stop making decisions for themselves and do what it takes to fit in.

Everyone in my school competes with each other. The kids with nice clothes and lots of money belong to this clique that looks down on the rest of us. It hurts that other people can make me feel inferior. I know they're not better than me, but everyone in school—even the teachers—treat them like they are.

Mandee, age 18[4]

It is not easy to cope with cliques. Teens who find supportive friends with similar interests, backgrounds, and morals can eliminate the pressure to conform to behavior they do not want to imitate. Teens should surround themselves with people who make them feel good about themselves and have fun at the same time.

I'm in a popular group at school, but lately my friends have been bugging me. All they want to do is party. I don't drink or fool around with lots of girls. My friends say, "You just don't know how to have a good time." It's not easy keeping my friends and my standards at the same time.

David, age 16[5]

Some young people find themselves left out or pressured because they will not participate in activities with a group. The kids who are engaging in the behavior may feel threatened or uncomfortable by those who do not. They may inwardly know that what they are doing is wrong and feel pressured to do it, anyway.[6] If a clique excludes people who do not do everything they do, it is not a good group to join. It is really just a whole bunch of difficult people. A good group is one that allows for individuality and encourages people to think and act for themselves. By making the right choice of friends, young people can avoid difficult situations . . . and the difficult people who cause them.

Teachers

Students are not the only difficult people at school. Sometimes a teacher's personality can be hard to handle. Although most teachers genuinely like their jobs and kids, there are teachers who are not nice or are simply "burned out." A difficult teacher is verbally critical of students, uses extreme punishments, or favors obvious "pets." If a teacher's attitude is so bad that it interferes with the learning environment, it should be brought to the teacher's attention. This can be done by a parent if the student feels intimidated. As with all classroom problems, it is always smart to talk to the teacher first. If this direct approach does not work, the principal should be notified. A truly inappropriate teacher does not belong in the classroom.

Most difficult teachers are not that bad. Teachers have different personalities, and it is part of the school experience to learn how to get along with a variety of people.

Students should remember that teachers are under a great deal of pressure instructing many young people each day. Their job is to share knowledge, not to be pals with their students. The student's job is to learn and to be respectful.

Saying please, thank you, sir, and ma'am may seem superficial, but it can give teachers the sense that they are being respected and appreciated.

My teachers hate me! Just because I'm not a perfect student, and sometimes I goof off in class. I can't help it if I'm bored. Isn't it their responsibility to keep me interested?

Zackary, age 14[7]

Some teachers are boring. Some subjects seem boring. But that does not give kids the right to be difficult students.

Sometimes school can seem boring. But that does not give kids the right to be difficult students.

In fact, a good student faced with an unpleasant class knows that being positive can change the whole situation. Instead of complaining or slacking off, good students find ways to make the topic easier or more fun. Teaming up with other students for study groups, finding creative ways to do assignments, and talking with adults who use this subject in their career are just a few ideas to spark enthusiasm.

My math teacher was so strict, and he gave us too much homework. I called him names to my friends and thought he was being mean. At the end of the year, I aced the state math exam. I realized that he was being hard on us to make us learn. Well, I learned that he wasn't a difficult teacher. I was a difficult student!

Katie, age 18[8]

Coping with different kinds of teachers prepares young people for the future when they will need to work with all kinds of people. School is a kind of training ground for the adult world—where there are difficult situations and difficult people, too. A student who learns to deal with problems in school has a solid foundation for success in the future.

5

Other Kids Can Be So Difficult!

ace it. Not everybody gets along with each other, and kids are no exception. Kids can drive each other crazy. When young people are difficult, it is usually when there are feelings that nobody admits or will talk about.[1] They may be feeling angry, threatened, insecure, shy, ashamed, jealous, frightened, and/or unloved, but they are not able to express themselves appropriately.[2] The source of the problem may be school, home, or their personality.

When another kid is difficult:

- ask him or her what is wrong and try to help
- talk to an adult about the problem
- avoid him or her

Here are some examples of ways kids can be difficult and some things that can be done to help.

Gossip

This girl was spreading rumors about me. I went straight to her to find out why she was saying these things. I told her to stop it. And she did! I'm glad I went straight to the source. I'm not so glad other kids chose to believe her without asking me if it were true.

Julie, age 17[3]

Some people cannot resist the temptation to talk about other people. Often, these stories provide a laugh at someone else's expense. If nobody encourages the gossiper or participates in spreading the tales, the person will not get the attention he or she desired. Stopping gossip means not participating in it.[4]

Know-It-All, Loudmouth, Class Clown

A kid in my class thinks he knows everything. He's such a brain, and he lets everyone know it.

Hector, age 13[5]

I wish Heather would just shut up sometimes. She's always talking, and she is so LOUD.

Katie, age 18[6]

Gregory is a funny guy, but he's never serious. It gets to be obnoxious—it's like he's always "on."

Zackary, age 14[7]

Kids who seek attention by grabbing the spotlight are often insecure and uneasy with themselves.[8] Their "look at me" behavior is a way to get reassurance and recognition. A helpful way to treat teens like that is with extra generosity. Complimenting them on their good qualities and giving them appreciation will help boost self-esteem. This makes the annoying behavior less necessary, since they are getting the praise they need. Of course, if they continue to be difficult it is acceptable to ignore them. Avoiding an annoying person is sometimes the only thing that works.

Prejudice

Brianna wouldn't play with me [when we were kids] because I'm a different race. I can't believe that in [this] century there are still racists.

Shenise, age 18[9]

Some people focus on others' differences and use these differences to ridicule, hurt, or attack others. A person who is prejudiced calls others names, makes jokes, excludes, teases, or judges others because of their skin color, religion, or culture.

People who are prejudiced need to understand that their actions hurt other people. Racism needs to be stopped. If somebody says something inappropriate, others should stand up to them and make it clear that this behavior will not be tolerated. If the hurtful words or actions persist, an adult should be informed.

Shy

I really like this boy, but he's so shy! He barely talks, and I don't know what to say to him.

Quinn, age 15[10]

Shy people are not trying to be difficult. But it can be difficult to be around them. To make shy people feel more comfortable, people can smile, make eye contact, encourage them to talk, and not tease them. It can be useful to prepare topics such as hobbies or music to keep the conversation from stalling.

When a Friend Is a Difficult Person

I've been friends with Helene since first grade. Lately, though, I want to be around her less and less. She's always got problems to complain about, and when I try to help her she doesn't take my advice. It's draining to be around her. She whines about her life but then doesn't do anything to change it.

Cindy, age 16[11]

My best friend is in big trouble. He got caught stealing a car. I know he was high at the time. Am I supposed to try to help him or stay away from him?

Peter, age 18[12]

Teenagers need to choose their friends with care and awareness. A difficult friend can range from annoying to dangerous. Problems such as stealing, alcohol/drug abuse,

There are less serious ways that friends can be difficult people. A difficult friend may:

- pressure others to do things they do not want to do or know they should not do
- act jealous, compete, put others down
- talk behind people's backs
- obsess over the opposite sex
- let boyfriends or girlfriends get in the way of friendship
- treat others disrespectfully or take them for granted

eating disorders, and depression are too big to be handled by young people. A friend whose personality or behavior is extreme or is causing continuous problems needs adult or professional help.

When a friend is difficult, it is important to look at the situation objectively. Do the bad or irritating times occur more often than the good times? Is this a friend who can be trusted? Are both parties willing to make an effort to make this friendship work? A healthy friendship is one that is easy and comfortable, not difficult and uncomfortable.

A good friend is honest, caring, and fun. When a friend has difficult moments, understanding and communication can help the friendship make it through the rough spots and grow stronger.

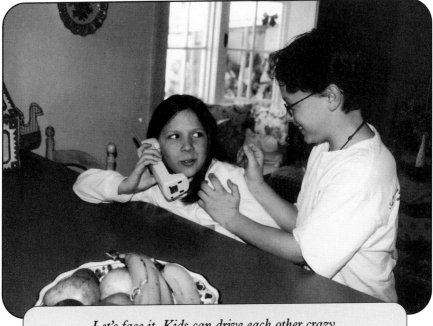

Let's face it. Kids can drive each other crazy.

Dating Difficult People

A healthy dating relationship is based on trust, respect, honesty, and safety. Teenagers who date are learning how to have a healthy relationship. Unfortunately, this process sometimes includes difficult dating experiences. Examples of unhealthy relationships are ones where there is cheating, jealousy, and/or abuse. Each of these can be reasons to break off a relationship immediately. A person who cheats or acts jealous is too difficult to date. A person who is abusive is also too dangerous to date.

Abuse

Abuse means acting in a way that is out of line—like sneering at someone who asks a simple question, or hitting someone for any reason at all. No one should ever tolerate any kind of abuse whether it comes from a boyfriend or girlfriend, adult, or partner of the same sex.

Types of Abuse

Physical abuse—is any contact that hurts the other person, including hitting, biting, grabbing, choking, and use of a weapon.

Verbal abuse—involves putting the other person down, swearing, making mean comments or threats, shouting, and name-calling.

Emotional abuse—is statements or behavior deliberately intended to hurt the other person. This includes ignoring, promising to do something and not following through, breaking dates, and withholding attention and affection.

Sexual abuse—is any bodily contact that is unwanted or hurtful—from hugging, kissing, or touching to forced intercourse.[13]

Date abuse is any hurtful or unwanted behavior. Date abuse can be physical, verbal, emotional, or sexual. This behavior should *never* be tolerated.

What to Do if You Have Been Abused

Find at least one adult to talk to. Tell a parent, teacher, school counselor, or someone else you trust. Call a hot line number.

Call the police if you think you might be in danger.

Try not to be alone. Ask someone to walk with you to and from school, work, and friends' homes.

There are other difficulties teens face when dealing with dating. Whether the problems are caused by immaturity, lack of communication, or personality conflicts, it is up to each partner to decide if the relationship should continue. Dating a difficult person is often not worth the time or energy it takes. Dating is meant to be enjoyable and comfortable—not difficult! A boyfriend or girlfriend who makes life more difficult is definitely not the right choice.

6

Difficult People . . . They Can Be Everywhere

ifficult people are not only found in school or at home. They can be everywhere, from the workplace to the road to the phone. Here are some examples of difficult people in the world, and what a person can do to help make them easier to deal with.

In the Workplace

Many young people work part-time after school and on weekends. Their jobs provide opportunities for extra spending money, work experience, and dealing with different kinds of people. Young employees learn interpersonal skills while working with supervisors, co-workers, and clients. When relationships between people at work run smoothly, so does the work day. When conflicts arise, work can become an unpleasant, or even miserable, experience.

Working for a difficult boss is a challenging experience. Even though someone is the boss, he or she is a human being. Bosses usually reach their positions because of their experience, education, and management skills. But they can feel insecure, pressured by business or personal lives, and tired. Some bosses use their power on the job to give them a false sense of self-worth. Others simply do not have the qualities that make an effective boss.

Difficult bosses look for people who can work *with* them and who can be counted on to work professionally. An employee who can adapt to the personality and to the management style of a difficult boss will be valued. The employee who handles a job and a difficult boss should pat himself or herself on the back. Along with a paycheck, he or she is gaining self-confidence and self-respect.

Working for a difficult boss is a challenging experience.

My boss drives me crazy sometimes because she's so picky. But it also makes me work harder and do the job right.

Amy, age 18[1]

There are situations that are completely unacceptable at work. Behaviors that are inappropriate include sexual harassment, improper humor, and illegal activity. Sexual harassment consists of words and actions that make another person uncomfortable. A sexual harasser may threaten to cause problems or fire someone if he or she does not go along with the behavior. Improper humor involves racial, religious, or sexual jokes. Illegal activity includes alcohol, drugs, unlawful use of money or power, and unsafe working conditions.

None of these situations should be tolerated. An employee (or employees, since there can be strength in numbers) should take immediate action. A good first step is to speak with the person who works at the next higher level. For example, an employee could go to a manager with

Recently, I quit my job at a pizza restaurant because of harassment. Another employee harassed me and another girl. She is going to court, and I'm going to be a witness. I'm nervous, but it's the right thing to do. But it really hurt that after one and a half years of working there, I was the one who had to leave and find a new job. The owner just wouldn't do anything about it.

Mandee, age 17[2]

A girl at work kept pinching my rear end. Finally, I said really loudly so everyone could hear, "Stop pinching my butt. I don't want you to touch me." She was really embarrassed, and she never did it again.

Dylan, age 16[3]

a problem about an assistant manager. Sometimes, however, there is no higher-up. If the big boss or company owner is the problem, another adult must be notified. Whether it is a parent, teacher, or police officer, somebody outside the situation must be told. If the problem is too bad or is not resolved quickly, the employee should quit. Continuing to work in a bad environment is unnecessary, and it may even be dangerous.

Steps to Take in a Difficult Work Situation

- Speak directly to the person causing the problem
- Speak to a higher-up
- File a report or formal complaint
- Tell an adult, parent, teacher, or police officer
- Quit and find a better place to work

Dealing With a Difficult Customer

Not only bosses or co-workers can be difficult, but customers may also be difficult to please. In such a situation:

- apologize when necessary
- ask for the facts
- listen carefully
- accept responsibility
- promise to take specific steps to correct the situation
- try not to take insults personally
- call a manager or supervisor the minute the customer begins to lose control or acts inappropriately[4]

On the Internet

Difficult people are not encountered only in person anymore. They can be found on the computer when using the Internet. Young people today must be cybersmart. Nobody using an Internet chat room or bulletin board should ever give out information identifying him or her. A person who offers his or her name, address, school, phone number, or parent's workplace could be sending out an unsafe message to the wrong person. Although many perfectly nice, normal people are online, there are also plenty of dangerous people. A person who seems friendly may really be a pedophile (an adult who sexually preys on young people) or mentally unstable.

Young people today must be especially cybersmart.

Good ways to prevent and avoid difficult situations on the Internet include using it with adult supervision, sticking to kid-friendly, established sites, and e-mailing only people who are personal friends and family members. If a person is bothersome, the teen should log off the Internet, or at least get out of the chat room or Instant Message situation. On some computer systems, a person can block instant messages or e-mail from anyone with whom he or she does not want to speak. Disconnecting somebody who causes uncomfortable feelings is not rude. It is smart. If the person continues to be difficult by sending unwanted e-mails or instant messages, the user should forward copies of the messages to the online service provider. They are responsible for assisting customers who are having trouble and can deal properly with the offender.

My mom makes sure I'm really careful when I go online. She'd never, ever let me meet a total stranger that I met over the Internet. You never really know who it is you're talking to.

Quinn, age 15[5]

Difficult Drivers

The news is filled with stories about automobile accidents and incidences of road rage. Difficult drivers include people who are impatient, angry, elderly, or driving under the influence of drugs or alcohol. The best way to deal with a person who is acting badly behind the wheel is to stay calm and get far away from him or her. Getting angry or trying to change another driver's behavior can cause many more problems than it solves. The only thing on the road more dangerous than one irrational driver is two irrational drivers.[6] If someone driving another vehicle appears dangerous, a responsible driver should pull off at the nearest side street or exit and notify the police. Under no circumstances should somebody take matters into his own hands. This could lead to violence or an accident, which is exactly what most people hope to prevent. The Department of Motor Vehicles, insurance companies, and travel agencies teach traffic safety and defensive driving classes. Young people who are educated are best prepared to deal with difficult driving situations—and the people who cause them.

> *Never, never get in a car with a driver who has been drinking, even a little bit. Get his or her keys, call your parents, call the police. As the commercial says, "Friends don't let friends drive drunk."*

> Zackary, age 14[7]

Dealing With Telemarketers

Telemarketers are salespeople who call up customers on the phone and try to market their goods that way. Sometimes they can be annoying, especially when they call right at dinnertime. To discourage a telemarketer, try these techniques:

- Hang up immediately
- Say "Take me off your list" politely and hang up
- If the telemarketer calls back, ask for the manager's name and tell the person that an attorney will take action if the calls continue

Difficult Strangers

Young people come into contact with strangers in public places such as shopping malls, concerts, buses, or sidewalks. Even when strangers become difficult, it is best not to get into a conflict. The person may have a mental illness, be under the influence of drugs or alcohol, be hiding a weapon, or become physically violent. Dealing with a difficult stranger means ignoring the person, moving far away from him or her, and getting help from an adult if necessary.

The world, unfortunately, is not always a safe place. Difficult people are out there. Being aware and prepared makes sense in today's environment.

7

Getting Along With a Difficult Person

From the moment we are born, we begin learning about living with other people. With our words and actions we begin to sense how others react to us and how we react to other people.

Eda LeShan[1]

When dealing with difficult people, there is always a choice. In fact, there are four choices:

- Stay and do nothing
- Walk away from the situation
- Change behavior
- Change attitude[2]

The first option is not very constructive. Letting a difficult person continue his or her behavior tends to prolong the suffering and build up frustration. This is a short-term option, not a long-term solution. Leaving the situation is the right choice in certain situations. Not all problems can be resolved in the heat of the moment. If everything being said is making matters worse, or if one or both parties is losing control, walk away.

A change in behavior causes the other person to learn new ways of dealing with a situation. Doing something different forces a different response.

I was being picked on by a group of kids in my dance class. One day, instead of getting upset, I walked up to the girl who bugged me most. I said, "You do this step better than anyone. Would you show me how to do it right?" She was shocked, but she helped me. After that, she and the other girls were nicer to me. I think I surprised the meanness out of them!

Cindy, age 16[3]

If what you're doing obviously isn't working, do something else!

Julie, age 17[4]

Finally, a change in attitude always helps when dealing with a difficult person. Frustration, resentment, and anger are normal emotions to feel in the circumstances. However, switching to a different perspective can make the whole situation seem different.

My dad told me he had to miss my game because of work, and instead of yelling at him I told him it was okay. I remembered all the games he did come to and told him I appreciated his working so hard to support the family. He was really happy to hear that, and I felt better too.

Dylan, age 16[5]

Compliments and appreciation can bring out the best instead of the "beast." By reinforcing the positive, a difficult person seems less troublesome.

Learning to see humor in a difficult situation also helps.[6] A sense of humor can defuse a difficult person's temper and lighten up everybody's attitudes.

My brother and I were fighting at the dinner table. It was over something dumb, but I was really getting furious. Suddenly, my brother peeled two slices of pepperoni off his pizza and stuck them to his eyeballs. He looked so silly I had to laugh. It made me realize how stupid our argument really was, and we ended up just giggling for the rest of the meal.

Daphne, age 19[7]

Communication

When dealing with a difficult person, communication is very important. Communication involves spoken words, tone of voice, and body language. People respond to both verbal and nonverbal messages. A person who shouts, points his finger, moves too close, or uses curse words comes across as aggressive. Someone who crosses his or her arms, turns away, or speaks in monosyllables appears uncooperative. But a person who smiles, sits down, or speaks calmly and politely is showing that he or she is willing to communicate.

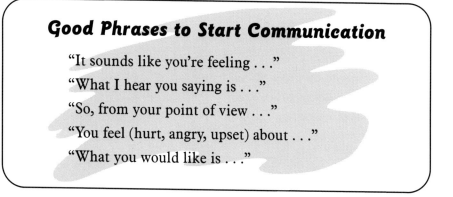

Good Phrases to Start Communication

"It sounds like you're feeling . . ."

"What I hear you saying is . . ."

"So, from your point of view . . ."

"You feel (hurt, angry, upset) about . . ."

"What you would like is . . ."

The goal of communicating with a difficult person is to end with both people feeling like winners. By listening carefully to what the other person is saying, trying to understand his feelings, and compromising when appropriate, a difficult situation can often be worked out. These skills require patience and effort, but they certainly can pay off in the long run.

Be Prepared

There are things people can do to be prepared for occasions when somebody becomes difficult. Planning behaviors and responses in advance can help resolve a sticky situation smoothly.

A person who shouts, moves too close, or uses curse words comes across as aggressive.

Preparing to Deal With a Difficult Person

- Practice/rehearse possible things to say in front of a mirror
- Ask family and/or friends for advice and support
- Decide what attitude to convey: confidence, calmness, patience, determination, caring
- Practice deep breathing techniques to reduce stress and keep the mind clear
- Learn martial arts for self-confidence and self-defense[8]

Conclusion

Nobody has the right to mistreat another person or treat another without respect. And no one should put up with being mistreated. Learning to deal with difficult people is a skill that will make life easier. Each time a difficult situation is avoided or resolved is an accomplishment. The rewards for success are self-confidence, self-respect, and peace!

I've learned that I can't fix every person or solve every problem, but I am responsible for my own actions. I try to stand up for myself and not let other people treat me jerky. If somebody gets mad at me because I won't let them get away with it, that's their choice. I just can't let someone else affect the way I see myself.

Peter, age 18[9]

Somebody I know at school was being a pain over and over again. Finally, I said, "Don't do that anymore." She gave me a hard time for the last time, and now there's one less difficult person in my life!

Amy, age 18[10]

A difficult situation resolved in a peaceful way is always an accomplishment.

Chapter Notes

Chapter 1. What Is a Difficult Person?

1. Personal interview with Julie, December 1999.
2. Brandon Torporov, *The Complete Idiot's Guide to Getting Along With Difficult People* (New York: Alpha Books, 1997), p. 9.
3. Personal interview with Zackary, November 1999.
4. Personal interview with David, December 1999.
5. Personal interview with Amy, October 1999.

Chapter 2. How Difficult People Can Make You Feel

1. Personal interview with Hector, November 1999.
2. Personal interview with Katie, November 1999.
3. Personal interview with Shenise, October 1999.
4. Personal interview with Amy, October 1999.
5. Personal interview with Dylan, December 1999.
6. Gary and Greg Smalley, *Bound by Honor* (Wheaton, Ill.: Tyndale House Publishers, 1998), p. 59.
7. Personal interview with David, December 1999.

Chapter 3. When Parents Are Difficult

1. Personal interview with Zackary, November 1999.
2. Personal interview with Cindy, December 1999.
3. Dr. Paul Meier, *Don't Let the Jerks Get the Best of You* (Nashville, Tenn.: Thomas Nelson Publishers, 1993), p. 143.
4. Eda Leshan, *When Kids Drive You Crazy— How to Get Along With Your Friends and Enemies* (New York: Penguin Books, 1990), p. 67.
5. Ibid., p. 58.
6. David Knox, *Choices in Relationships: An Introduction to Marriage and the Family*, 4th ed. (St. Paul, Minn.: West Publishing Co., 1994), pp. 598–599.
7. Personal interview with Cindy, December 1999.
8. Personal interview with Peter, October 1999.

9. Janet Dight, *Do Your Parents Drive You Crazy?* (New York: Prentice Hall Press, 1987), p. 31.

10. Lawrence Kutner, Ph.D., *Making Sense of Your Teenager* (New York: William Morrow and Co., 1997), p. 53.

11. Ibid., p. 27.

12. Charles E. Schaefer, Ph.D. and Theresa Foy Digeronimo, M.Ed., *How to Talk to Teens About Really Important Things* (San Francisco: Jossey-Bass, 1999), p. 1.

13. Barbara Meltz, *Put Yourself in Their Shoes* (New York: Dell Publishing, 1999), p. 14.

14. Personal interview with Daphne, November 1999.

15. Dight, p. 20.

16. Personal interview with Hector, December 1999.

17. Personal interview with Shenise, October 1999.

18. Personal interview with Quinn, October 1999.

19. Dight, p. 64.

20. Personal interview with Dylan, December 1999.

21. Personal interview with Cindy, December 1999.

Chapter 4. Difficult School Situations

1. Amy Dickinson, "Personal Time, Your Family: Bully Pulpit," August 30, 1999, <http://www.time.com/time/personal19990830/family.html> (October 25, 2000).

2. Richard Cohen, *Students Resolving Conflict* (Glenview, Ill.: Goodyear Books, 1995), p. 1.

3. Eda Leshan, *When Kids Drive You Crazy—How to Get Along With Your Friends and Enemies* (New York: Penguin Books, 1990), p. 9.

4. Personal interview with Mandee, October 1999.

5. Personal interview with David, December 1999.

6. Dianna Daniels Dooher, *Making Friends With Yourself and Other Strangers* (New York: Simon and Schuster, 1982), p. 181.

7. Personal interview with Zackary, November 1999.

8. Personal interview with Katie, November 1999.

Chapter 5. Other Kids Can Be So Difficult!

1. Eda Leshan, *When Kids Drive You Crazy—How to Get Along With Your Friends and Enemies* (New York: Penguin Books, 1990), p. 9.

2. Ibid., p. 11.

3. Personal interview with Julie, December 1999.

4. Dianna Daniels Dooher, *Making Friends With Yourself and Other Strangers* (New York: Simon and Schuster, 1982), p. 154.

5. Personal interview with Hector, December 1999.

6. Personal interview with Katie, November 1999.

7. Personal interview with Zackary, November 1999.

8. Dooher, p. 64.

9. Personal interview with Shenise, October 1999.

10. Personal interview with Quinn, October 1999.

11. Personal interview with Cindy, December 1999.

12. Personal interview with Peter, October 1999.

13. Barrie Levy and Patricia Griggans, *What Parents Need to Know about Dating Violence* (Seattle, Wash.: Seal Press, 1995), pp. 3–9.

Chapter 6. Difficult People . . . They Can Be Everywhere

1. Personal interview with Amy, October 1999.

2. Personal interview with Mandee, October 1999.

3. Personal interview with Dylan, December 1999.

4. Brandon Torporov, *The Complete Idiot's Guide to Getting Along With Difficult People* (New York: Alpha Books, 1997), p. 7.

5. Personal interview with Quinn, October 1999.

6. Torporov, p. 298.

7. Personal interview with Zackary, November 1999.

Chapter 7. Getting Along With a Difficult Person

1. Eda Leshan, *When Kids Drive You Crazy—How to Get Along With Your Friends and Enemies* (New York: Penguin Books, 1990), p. 12.

2. Drs. Rick Brinkman and Rick Kirschner, *Dealing with People You Can't Stand* (New York: McGraw-Hill, 1994), p. 12.

3. Personal interview with Cindy, December 1999.

4. Personal interview with Julie, December 1999.

5. Personal interview with Dylan, December 1999.

6. Dianne Daniels Dooher, *Making Friends With Yourself and Other Strangers* (New York: Simon and Schuster, 1982), pp. 144–145.

7. Personal interview with Daphne, November 1999.

8. Brinkman, p. 8.

9. Personal interview with Peter, October 1999.

10. Personal interview with Amy, October 1999.

Further Reading

Adler, Patricia and Peter Adler. *Peer Power: Preadolescent Culture & Identity*. New Brunswick, N.J.: Rutgers University Press, 1998.

Bell, Arthur H. *Winning With Difficult People*. Minneapolis, Minn.: Fairview Press, 1996.

Berent, Irwin M. and Rod L. Evans. *The Right Words: The Three Hundred Fifty Best Things to Say to Get Along With People*. New York: Warner Books, 1992.

Board, John C. *Special Relationship: Our Teachers and How We Learn*. Scranton, Penn.: W. W. Norton, 1991.

Cohen, Richard. *Students Resolving Conflict: Peer Mediation in Schools*. Reading, Mass.: Addison-Wesley Educational Publishers, Inc., 1995.

Daniels, Aubrey C. *Bringing Out the Best in People*. New York: McGraw-Hill, 2000.

Felder, David W. *Teenage Conflicts: Role Play Peacegames*. Tallahassee, Fla.: Wellington Press, 1995.

Henkart, Andrea F. *Cool Communication: A Mother & Daughter Reveal the Keys to Mutual Understanding Between Parents & Kids*. New York: Putnam, 1998.

King, Claudia. *Life Mastery: A Self-Esteem Handbook for Adults & Children*. Chico, Calif.: Light Paths Communication, 1994.

Kransnow, Janice. *How to Get Along With Other People*. Barrytown, N.Y.: Station Hill Press, 1995.

Lundin, William and Kathleen Lundin. *Working With Difficult People*. Saranac Lakes, N.Y.: Amacom, 1995.

McEwan, Elaine K. *How to Deal With Parents Who Are Angry, Troubled, Afraid, or Just Plain Crazy.*Thousand Oaks, Calif.: Corwin Press, 1998.

Nathan, Amy. *Everything You Need to Know about Conflict Resolution.* New York: Rosen Publishing Group, 1999.

Simpson, Carolyn. *Coping Through Conflict Resolution & Peer Mediation.* Center City, Minn.: Hazelden Information & Educational Services, 1998.

Solomon, Muriel. *Getting What You Want and Deserve From . . . Rotten Bosses, Demanding Spouses, Phony Friends, Preying Parents, Annoying Neighbors & Other Irritating People.* Nashville, Tenn.: Rutledge Hill Press, 1999.

Wandberg, Robert. *Conflict Resolution: Communication, Cooperation, Compromise.* Mankato, Minn.: Capstone Press, Inc., 2000.

Internet Sites

Drug and Alcohol Abuse

Substance Abuse and Mental Health Services Administration

<http://www.samhsa.gov>

The National Clearinghouse for Alcohol and Drug Information online, with a special emphasis on prevention and how teens can help when there is a problem.

Sexual Abuse

PANdora's Box

<http://www.prevent-abuse-now.com>

Information on the nature of child sexual abuse, as well as how to prevent and report abuses.

Dating

Breakup Girl to the Rescue

<http://breakup-girl.com>

A teen guide to relationships—the before, during, and after.

Love & Friendship

<http://www.smartgirl.org/index.html>

Advice on how to deal with crushes, relationships, and breaking up.

Peer Mediation

School Mediation Associates

<http://www.schoolmediation.com/index.html>

Provides resources to help manage school-based conflicts effectively.

Bullies

The Review Zone

<http://www.thereviewzone.com/bullies.html>

An article called "Bullies Are a Pain in the Brain," which gives a light-hearted but serious look at how to deal with bullies.

Safe Child Program Bullies Page

<http://www.safechild.org>

A program to prevent bullying when possible. Also includes information for parents on what to do if your child is being bullied, or is the bully.

Index